PHRASES, CLAUSES, *and* CONJUNCTIONS

ANN RIGGS

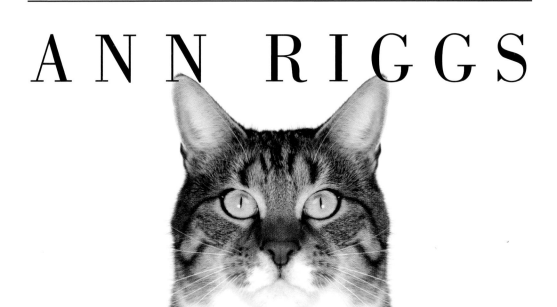

CREATIVE ☙ EDUCATION

Published by Creative Education
P.O. Box 227, Mankato, Minnesota 56002
Creative Education is an imprint of The Creative Company
www.thecreativecompany.us

Design and production by Liddy Walseth
Art direction by Rita Marshall
Printed by Corporate Graphics in the United States of America

Photographs by Photographs by Corbis (Hulton-Deutsch Collection), Getty Images
(Archive Photos, Anne Frank Fonds-Basel/Anne Frank House-Amsterdam, Michael Blann,
Tobi Corney, Kim Sayer, Kim Taylor, Tom and Steve), iStockphoto
(Jill Battaglia, Andrea Gingerich, Eileen Hart, Hypergon, Eric Isselée, Guillermo Lobo,
Chris Price, Steve Snowden, Srdjan Srdjanov, Syagci, James Trice)

Library of Congress Cataloging-in-Publication Data
Riggs, Ann.
Phrases, clauses and conjunctions / by Ann Riggs.
p. cm. — (Understanding grammar)
Includes bibliographical references and index.
Summary: An examination of the rules behind English grammar, focusing on the components known as phras-
es, clauses, and conjunctions, which are groups of words that comprise and connect all parts of a sentence.
ISBN 978-1-60818-094-3
1. English language—Terms and phrases. 2. English language—Clauses. 3. English language—Conjunctions.
4. English language—Grammar. I. Title. II. Series.

PE1689.R47 2010
428.2—dc22 2010028302

CPSIA: 110310PO1386

First Edition
2 4 6 8 9 7 5 3 1

TABLE of CONTENTS

Music swells. Siblings squabble. Owls hoot. I am. Grammar is. And just like

that, two words can become a SENTENCE. The information in a short sentence can be

expanded by adding more words that give vivid descriptions or specific reactions.

Where should those words be placed? How does a writer know what PUNCTUATION to

use? What does all of that mean, anyway? Words fall into place more easily when one

has an understanding of grammar, a system of rules that gives writers the foundation

for producing acceptable, formal expression. It is that acceptable form, that appropri-

ate grammar, which helps readers comprehend what has been written.

Basic sentences have a subject (someone or something) and a PREDICATE or verb (action

or state of being). Within sentences are groups of words called phrases and clauses.

A phrase is a group of related words without subject and verb that acts like one PART

OF SPEECH, such as the phrase "in the meantime" (which acts like an adverb, or a

word that describes a verb) or the expression "spill the beans" (phrasal verb) or the

description "hovering in the branches" (adjective). How are the words related? Al-

though each word is still its own part of speech, the group functions as a unit.

[4]

Clauses are different from phrases in that they have a subject and a verb. A sentence may have one clause or several, but the minimum requirement is one, since all clauses—and all sentences—need to have at least one group of words with a subject and a verb. When a clause can stand by itself and make sense, it's called independent. When it cannot exist on its own, it's called dependent and often needs the help of a connecting word, a conjunction, to attach it to a MAIN CLAUSE.

Conjunctions can coordinate, SUBORDINATE, and CORRELATE, but whatever they do, they always make phrases and clauses communicate within and between sentences. Without all three parts—phrases, additional clauses, and conjunctions—our sentences would all have the same stark structure: one clause of one subject and one verb. Adding other words gives writers a way to increase variety in their work and bring sentences to life!

FLAWLESS PHRASES

One of the most common types of phrases is the prepositional phrase. In it, a preposition with its noun or pronoun OBJECT relates to another word in the sentence, as in this example with the common prepositions *from* and *for*: **This is *from* me *for* you.** The rules of grammar state that a preposition should appear right next to its object (as with the previous objects, "me" and "you") and that a sentence should never end with a preposition. But sometimes it's acceptable to bend the rules in order to make

PREPOSITIONS

about	above	across	after	against
along	amid	among	around	as
at	before	behind	below	beneath
beside	besides	between	beyond	but (meaning except)
by	concerning	considering	despite	down
during	except	excepting	excluding	for
from	in	in front of	inside	into
like	near	of	off	on
onto	opposite	outside	over	past
per	regarding	since	than	through
throughout	to	together with	toward	towards
under	underneath	unlike	until	up
upon	via	with	within	without

TABLE 1

the sentence sound more like natural speech. Here's an example: **She's not the person I talked *with*.** Although we're ending a sentence with a preposition, it is less formal and easier to understand than this: **She's not the person *with* whom I talked.** Likewise, saying, **Where did that come *from*?** instead of ***From* where did that come?** fits better into a conversation. It is never permissible, however, to end a sentence with an unnecessary preposition: **Where is he *at*?** or **Where did she go *to*?** Before we go on, see Table 1 above for a review of commonly used prepositions.

Prepositional phrases have many functions within sentences, but their most important job is building relationships between words. One way to identify a prepositional phrase is to find the sentence's subject and verb and then see what's left. In *The Indian in the Cupboard* (1980) by British author Lynne Banks (1929–), Omri, the main character, encounters (and attempts to conceal from his family) toys that come alive. Find the 15 prepositional phrases in the short excerpt on the following page.

" Breakfast in his house was often a dicey [un-predictable] meal anyway, with everybody more or less bad-tempered.... Under cover of the moans that went up about the prospect of no apples in the autumn, and the exclamations about the size of the hailstones, Omri slipped his coat on and ran through the bouncing ice lumps to school. On the way he stopped under a protecting yew tree and took the little men out. He showed them each a large hailstone, which, to them, was the size of a football. "

The main parts of those sentences are:

Breakfast was often a dicey meal anyway. Omri slipped his coat on and ran. He stopped and took the little men out. He showed them each a large hailstone, which was the size.

The last part doesn't make much sense without the ending prepositional phrase, "*of* a football," does it? We have found the action, but all the details and relationships are missing! In the first sentence, "*in* his house" modifies, or describes, "breakfast," while "*with* everybody more or less bad-tempered," tells more about the noun, "meal." When "*Under* cover" tells us how Omri got out of his house, "*of* the moans ... and the exclamations" tells us what kind of "cover" he had. The three phrases "*about* the prospect," "*of* no apples," and "*in* the autumn" tell more about each other and give more information about the sentence as a whole. Similarly, the next phrases in line are integral to understanding the entire sentence: Without "*of* the hailstones," the description "*about* the size" doesn't make sense. And if we take out both phrases, we have no clue why anyone is exclaiming at all. The sentence ends by describing where Omri ran: "*through* the bouncing ice lumps" and "*to* school." In the next sentence, we know when and where Omri stopped: "*On* the way" and "*under* a protecting yew tree." Finally, the last sentence ends with "*to* them," an object phrase, and "*of* a football," a descriptive phrase about the hailstone. Who knew prepositions and their objects could relate to other words in so many different ways!

Prepositional phrases make up only one kind of word group. Three types of verb forms called verbals can also make phrases. Verbals may look like verbs, but they can never function as the main verb of a sentence. A gerund is a verbal noun and can be used

in a sentence in all the ways a noun can. In the sentence, **I appreciate his *keeping me informed***, *keeping* is a gerund; "*keeping me informed*" is a gerund phrase, the direct object (a noun phrase that receives the action of a verb) of the verb "appreciate." Also of note in that example is the correct use of the possessive pronoun "his" before the gerund, showing ownership of the verbal, rather than the OBJECTIVE CASE, as in **I appreciate *him* keeping me informed.** The second type of verbal is the participle, which can also be used as an adjective. Notice the adjective phrase in this sentence: **The realtor *receiving* the most referrals will be rewarded.** The participle *receiving* is in the present TENSE, and "*receiving* the most referrals" is the participial phrase modifying "realtor." The third verbal, an infinitive, is defined as "*to* and a verb." Infinitives can function as nouns or as modifiers. In the next example, the infinitive phrase is the subject of the sentence: **To be prepared for anything is a lofty ambition.** However, in **Abby felt an irresistible urge *to exercise*,** the infinitive *to exercise* acts as an adjective, describing the noun "urge."

See if you can find 10 prepositional phrases and 5 infinitives in the last paragraph from

United States president Abraham Lincoln's (1809–65) second INAUGURAL ADDRESS of March 4, 1865. Refer to the listing of prepositions in Table 1 if you need to, and remember, "*to* and a verb" makes an infinitive.

TO+VERB

" With malice toward none; with charity for all; with firmness in the right, as God gives us to see the right, let us strive on to finish the work we are in; to bind up the nation's wounds; to care for him who shall have borne the battle, and for his widow and his orphan—to do all which may achieve and cherish a just and lasting peace among ourselves, and with all nations. "

ABRAHAM LINCOLN,
REPUBLICAN CANDIDATE FOR PRESIDENT OF THE UNITED STATES.

The first four words make up two prepositional phrases; together, they describe how to "strive on." Similarly, "*with* charity" and "*for* all" are also coupled as one adverb, as are "*with* firmness" and "*in* the right." Phrases seven ("*for* him") and eight ("*for* his widow and his orphan") complete the "to care" infinitive phrase as nouns and a pronoun used as COMPOUND OBJECTS, while the last two ("*among* ourselves" and "*with* all nations") are used as adjectives that modify the noun "peace." Did you notice that the infinitive phrases also had prepositions with nouns or pronouns after them? Take another look at Lincoln's goals for the unified nation. If we removed all the prepositional and infinitive phrases, the result would be "as God gives us, let us strive on, and." That's not much to go on, is it? While it may not have been Lincoln's intent, he has given us an impressive grammar lesson in the importance of prepositional and infinitive phrases.

FOR HIS HIS WIDOW &HIS ORPHAN

Verbs—but Not

Fill in each blank with a verb that ends in *-ing*:

_____ IS GOOD EXERCISE.

SHARON ENJOYS _____ AT WORK.

MARTY'S FAVORITE PASTIME IS _____.

Your choices of a subject, a direct object, and a predicate nominative (a noun in the predicate that renames the subject) were all used as nouns—they were gerunds. This time write each of those *-ing* words in your own sentences, using them to describe someone or something. Your *-ing* verbs will now function as adjectives—they'll become participles. Finally, write three more sentences that correctly use infinitives ("*to* and a verb") as nouns or modifiers, such as this direct object: "Does the car need *to be washed*?"

FURTHER PHRASAL DIVERSITY

Other types of phrases connect certain components of a sentence to add meaning. Transitional phrases assist the writer in organizing thoughts, helping ideas flow smoothly from the first point to the last. They often begin with a preposition or an adverb. See Table 2 for some of the most common transitions.

During World War II (1939–45), a Jewish girl living in Holland received a diary for her 13th birthday. This became Anne Frank's amazing story of the two years she and her family were in hiding before they were captured by the police of Nazi Germany, the Gestapo. Find Anne's transition that contrasts one way of thinking with another in the following excerpt from an entry dated March 7, 1944.

TRANSITIONAL PHRASES

after all	as a result	at any rate
at the same time	by the way	even so
for example	in addition	in conclusion
in contrast	in fact	in other words
in the first place	on the contrary	on the other hand

TABLE 2

" I don't see how Mummy's idea can be right, because then how are you supposed to behave if you go through the misery yourself? Then you are lost. On the contrary, I've found that there is always some beauty left—in nature, sunshine, freedom, in yourself; these can all help you.... And whoever is happy will make others happy too. He who has courage and faith will never perish in misery! **"**

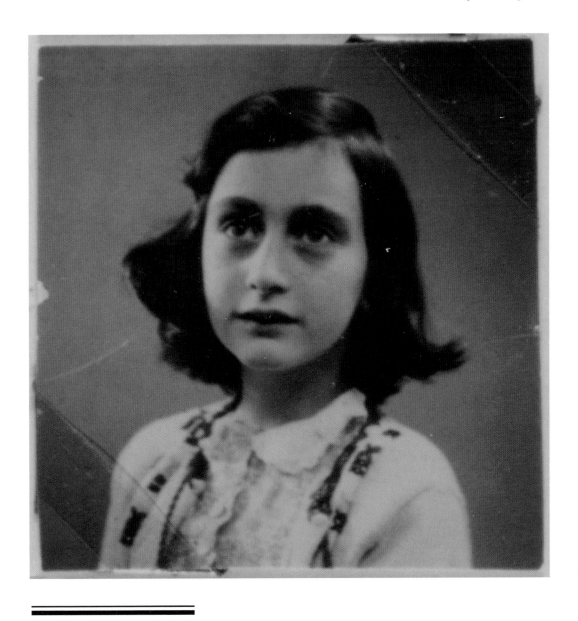

Anne Frank, pictured at age 13 in 1942

Do you hear the diarist's emphatic voice? After analyzing her mother's view, stating how she opposes it, Anne uses the transitional phrase, "on the contrary." Using the transition as she does, the reader is on the lookout for a contrasting view. Although Anne wasn't writing her diary for others to read, the form makes it easy to follow, and the relationship between the ideas is clear because of it.

Another phrase type, a PARTICIPIAL PREPOSITIONAL PHRASE, may seem like a contradiction in terms. While a participle is a verb form that can show action or modify a noun, it can also sometimes function as a preposition with an object: ***Considering the lateness of the hour, the chairman shortened the business meeting.*** In this way, a participial preposition can be substituted for a phrasal preposition, or two or more words used as one preposition. Instead of the phrase "with regard to," say "regarding," if you're talking about something like "the last item on the agenda."

The next phrase category is the familiar verb phrase. In this phrase, a main verb and a HELPING VERB are used as a unit, such as: **Ella *has broken* her wrist again; I *have looked* everywhere for that book**; and

The package *should have been delivered* yesterday. Writers need to pay particular attention to verb phrases to be sure they agree with subjects, matching singular helping verbs with singular subjects and plural helping verbs with plural subjects. And when *or* connects the parts of a COMPOUND SUBJECT, the subject closer to the verb determines the choice of the helper. The following example uses plural subject *buses* and plural verb *are*: **Either the early bus or the later *buses are* supposed to take all the equipment.** In the next sentence, however, the singular subject *sponsor* is nearer to the singular verb *is*: **The parents or the *sponsor is* going to sign the forms.** Verb phrases separated by an adverb modifier such as *not* may be trickier to identify, as in **They *have not heard* the end of this.** Just remember to find the action verb (*heard*) and then look for the helping verb (*have*).

As we've seen, there are many kinds of phrases, but each is a group of two or more words used for one purpose. Sometimes the phrase even acts as one word. A phrasal adjective, also known as a compound modifier, describes a noun and is often hyphenated:

WITH EMPHATIC VOICE!

A *state-inspected* facility has high standards; The *lower-than-expected* earnings surprised no one; and The recipe called for *three-fourths* cup brown sugar. Another phrase category, the phrasal adverb, has two or more words, but it functions as one adverb. Adverbs modify verbs, adjectives, and other adverbs by answering the questions of *how?*, *when?*, *where?*, *why?*, and *how much?*, as in the following examples: As a *result* of the vote, the measure failed (*why*); Dog toys were found *here and there* throughout the house (*where*). A compound adverb, while appearing as a single word, can be divided into at least two smaller words used together as one adverb: *other + wise* is *otherwise*; *further + more* is *furthermore*; and *not + with + standing* is *notwithstanding*.

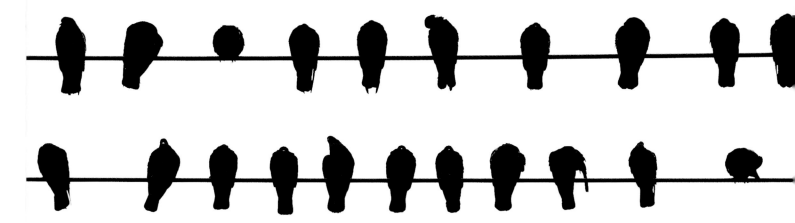

Finally, there is the phrasal verb, a group of words not defined by their original meanings. This category has a separate purpose; it isn't supposed be taken LITERALLY. Phrasal verbs can be made up of a verb and a preposition or adverb—or they can be made up of a preposition and an adverb—plus one or more nouns or pronouns. Here are some common expressions using phrasal verbs: to **back up** the hard drive, someone you can **count on**, going to **keep tabs on** you. Backing up the computer's hard drive (making another copy of the files) certainly doesn't mean you do that while walking backwards. And having a trusted friend has nothing to do with math problems, unless you're studying together. While an interest in keeping track of someone's activities may be important, attaching actual tags to the person is not called for.

Phrasal verbs are used in conversation and informal writing, and that's the key to our understanding them. Since we want to write acceptable, well-constructed sentences, we need to know what to avoid, as well as what is appropriate. When a person has been told

to **get over it** instead of "to try to resolve his feelings," the message is an IDIOM. Idiomatic phrasal verbs may also reflect certain dialects, or regional speech patterns. If someone says he's ready to **hang up his boots**, he's ready to retire from his job, not just put away his gear. Anybody who is told, **The ball is in your court now**, would need to understand that it's up to her to make a decision. And when a person wants to express a different opinion, perhaps putting himself in a tough position, he may begin by saying, **I'm going to go out on a limb here.** No gymnasium is in sight; no trees worthy of climbing are anywhere nearby; but the phrasal verbs make their unique meanings known. Such idioms are especially challenging to students learning English as a second language. In fact, the grammatical classification of phrasal verbs is often lost on native speakers as well! A dictionary is the best tool for learning phrasal verbs; try looking up a main verb such as "get" and see how many phrasal verb entries you can find. Beyond that, remember that idioms are generally not to be used in formal expression, such as the papers you write for school.

FORMING ALLIANCES

There are independent clauses, and then there are dependent (or subordinate) clauses. Words called conjunctions have different functions according to the types of clauses they join. Coordinating conjunctions (*and*, *or*, *but*, *for*, *nor*, *yet*, and *so*), the strongest of the connecting words, join independent clauses in sentences, other clauses, and words within clauses. A COMPOUND SENTENCE has two independent clauses connected with a coordinating conjunction, such as **Jan's family invited Beth to go with them on vacation, *but* she couldn't find anyone to work her shift that week.** Beginning a sentence with a coordinating conjunction is a way to add variety of expression. *And* it is permissible when the two sentences are closely related.

When a dependent clause needs help connecting to a main clause, we use a subordinating conjunction: ***If* the phone rings, don't answer it. Keep practicing *until* you can play that piece for your music teacher. Sid wants us to pick him up *because* his mom doesn't have a car this week.** As the previous example sentences show, clues for recognizing dependent clauses come from the words that introduce them. Table 3 on the opposite page is a helpful source for dependent clause clue words.

The conjunction *than* demands special attention when it begins a dependent clause in a sentence such as this one: **Stuart is taller *than* I.** You might be tempted to say, **Stuart is taller *than* me,** but you'd be wrong.

SUBORDINATING CONJUNCTIONS

after	although	as far as/ soon as	as if/even if	because
before	how	now/now that	once	since
than	that/so that	then	though/as though	until
when/ whenever	where/ wherever	whether	while	why

TABLE 3

THAT

Why? One part of that sentence can stand alone: **Stuart is taller.** But the subordinating conjunction *than* means the sentence has both an independent and a dependent clause. The tricky part is that the dependent part of the sentence is an incomplete comparison—it isn't all there. In our example, "than I" really thought. Many dependent clauses function in the sentence as adverbs that modify verbs, adjectives, or other adverbs. *That*, *which*, and *where* can begin clauses of more than one kind, though, and may be adjectives or adverbs, depending on the purpose of the clause in the sentence.

WHICH

means "than I am." Adding "am" clarifies the relationship of the verb with its subject pronoun "I." The object pronoun "me" has no place in the comparison.

The subordinate clause is a sentence FRAGMENT if left unconnected to an independent clause, so always join the dependent and independent clauses to make a complete

Keeping the word clues in mind, see if you can figure out what the following sentences have in common:

(1) If I only had an hour to chop down a tree, I would spend the first 45 minutes sharpening my axe.

(2) My father taught me to work; he did not teach me to love it.

WHERE

For one thing, Abraham Lincoln, who certainly knew about hard work, is given credit for having said them both. Second, in each of the complete sentences there is also an independent clause. Third, between the beginning capital letter and the ending period in each sentence are two groups of words with a subject and verb. For our purposes, that's where the similarities end. Considering the first sentence as a whole, *if* is a clue that the words before the comma are dependent upon the main clause for support. Even with its subject (*I*), verb (*had*), direct object (*hour*), infinitive (*to chop*), and prepositional phrase (*down* a tree), the beginning *if* makes the clause subordinate—dependent. The comma after "tree" shows where that subordinate clause ends. What "I" (Lincoln—subject) "would spend" (verb) 45 minutes doing is the part of the sentence that can stand alone; it's the independent clause.

Sentence two has a different punctuation clue; this time it's a semicolon that ends the first independent clause and shows where the second one begins. Both parts of the second sentence are independent and can make sense on their own: in the first part, the subject is "father" and the verb is "taught"; in the second part, the subject is "he" and the verb is "did ... teach." Because they are related by Lincoln's having mentioned his father and the subject of work, both independent clauses can be in the same compound sentence.

Relative clauses are dependent. They're called relative because they relate, or establish ties, to the independent, main clause of the sentence. The first word of a relative clause is a relative pronoun (*that, what, which, who, whoever, whom, whose*). The relative clause may be used as a subject, a direct object, an object of a preposition, or an appositive (a word that follows a noun, renaming and supplying more information about it). In **The puppy *that* Cheryl chased didn't have a collar,** the subordinate clause "*that* Cheryl chased" is used as an appositive and gives more information about the subject noun, "puppy." It is possible to be more concise and omit the relative pronoun *that*, since the meaning of the sentence is clearly understood; this is known as an elliptical (meaning something has been left out) construction: **The puppy Cheryl chased didn't have a collar.** The important thing to remember is to relate the main clause to the subordinate clause and that this is often done with a relative pronoun.

BUILD YOUR OWN SENTENCE
A Healthy Perspective

 According to Richard Carlson (1961–2006), American author of *Don't Sweat the Small Stuff for Teens* (2000), thinking more about what's right with your life than what's wrong with it can be a helpful and healthy habit to form. In the previous sentence, the subordinating conjunction *than* was a clue for a dependent clause. Try integrating some subordinating conjunctions into your own writing. Using at least five words from Table 3 on page 25 to tie the clauses in your sentences together, write about a positive person whom you know and how his or her outlook has affected you. Why is this person's optimism a trait you would want to pass on to others?

KNOWING ALL THE ANGLES

To see how a writer can benefit from an understanding of the various kinds of phrases, clauses, and conjunctions, look at this excerpt from *Gifted Hands: The Ben Carson Story* (1990), by surgeon Ben Carson (1951–). As you read the compelling information given in this nonfiction account of a young girl's struggle with seizures, notice the clue words for prepositional phases, dependent clauses, and conjunctions. See if you can identify the conjunctive adverb (page 34) in the first sentence.

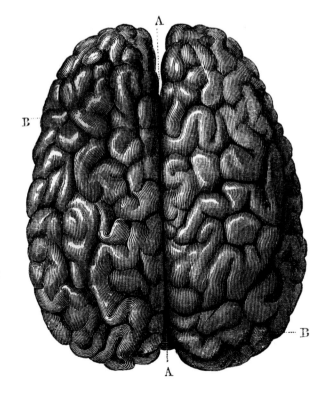

[38]

"Although born normal, Maranda Francisco had her first grand mal seizure at 18 months, a convulsion characteristic of epilepsy that we sometimes call an electrical storm in the brain. Two weeks later Maranda suffered a second grand mal seizure, and her doctor put her on anticonvulsive medication.

By her fourth birthday, the seizures were becoming more frequent. They also changed, suddenly affecting only the right side of her body. She didn't lose consciousness; the seizures were focal (half a grand mal), originating in the left side of her brain and disrupting only the right side of her body. Each seizure left Maranda weak on her right side, sometimes unable to talk normally for as long as two hours. By the time I heard about her situation, Maranda was experiencing up to 100 seizures a day, as often as three minutes apart, making the right side of her body useless…. Only during sleep was she seizure-free….

Maranda manages well without the left half of her brain because of a phenomenon we call plasticity. We know that the two halves of the brain aren't as rigidly divided as we once thought. Although both have distinct functions, one side has the major responsibility for language and the other for artistic ability. But children's brains have a considerable overlap. In plasticity, functions once governed by a set of cells in the brain are taken over by another set of cells. No one understands exactly how this works."

A conjunctive adverb phrase, ***Although* born normal,** leads into the main clause of sentence one, which features a prepositional phrase that tells when Maranda's first seizure occurred. In the dependent *that* clause of sentence one, another prepositional phrase acts as an adjective telling what kind of "characteristic," while **in the brain,** describing "storm," ends the clause. Sentence two begins with a phrasal adverb **two weeks *later*** that modifies the verb "suffered." The comma after "seizure" marks the end of the first independent clause, and with the coordinating conjunction *and*, the second independent clause begins. Within that clause is the important information contained in the prepositional phrase ***on* anticonvulsive medication.**

Do you recognize the first word of sentence three and its part of speech? ***By* her fourth birthday** begins with a preposition, and the phrase functions as an adverb telling when. Sentence four varies the construction by having the independent clause first, followed by a phrasal adverb, ***suddenly* affecting only the right side of her body.** That phrase tells how the seizures changed, and it ends with an adjective prepositional phrase ***of* her body** that describes "side."

Going on to sentence five, we can spot a punctuation clue in the semicolon after "consciousness" that divides the two independent clauses. The compound participial phrases with prepositional phrases are joined by the coordinating conjunction *and*. Which words are the participles in those phrases, words that look like verbs but are used as adjectives to modify "seizures"? They're the adjective *-ing* words, "originating" and "disrupting." Participles are something we haven't seen before in this excerpt. Look at sentence six to find something else. In the middle of the sentence is the infinitive phrase ***to talk* normally,** describing what Maranda is unable to do. It acts as an adverb saying how the seizures affect her.

Every sentence of Carson's explanation contains phrases, clauses, and usually a connecting word or two, making it possible to dissect this excerpt as thoroughly as a doctor might examine a brain! Sentence eight adds variety in beginning with an adverb (*only*), followed by a prepositional phrase (*during sleep*) also used as an adverb, as well as in reversing the order of the subject (*she*) and verb (*was*). Putting the verb first usually happens in an interrogative sentence (when the writer is asking a question), but here the reversed word order points to something the author feels is most important: the hyphenated phrasal adjective, *seizure-free.*

Dependent clauses outnumber independent ones in sentence 10, since the only words that can stand alone are the first 2, "We know." Let's look more closely at the dependent clause beginning with *that*. It is a clause, so it needs a subject and a verb: *halves* (subject) and *are* (verb; "aren't" includes the adverb "not").

WRITE THAT WAS REALLY WORTH SAYING?

easier it is for us to try them out for ourselves. However, it's one thing to study a writing style and just try to mimic it; it's an entirely different task to fill a blank page with correct grammar and expression of our own. Think about it this way: Other writers can be our support team. We can study their techniques and, by doing so, try to make what we say more effective. When we understand the process of using appropriate words, phrases, clauses, and conjunctions to write good sentences, we can concentrate on our ideas instead of each specific word.

What have we learned about in this book that may help our writing? Let's look at the lengthy list: prepositional phrases; verbal phrases—gerunds, participles, and infinitives; participial prepositions; verb phrases; phrasal adjectives and adverbs; phrasal verbs;

transitions; independent and dependent clauses (including relative clauses); elliptical constructions; and coordinating, subordinating, correlative, and adverb conjunctions. Although learning all of these names and functions can seem daunting at first, understanding these pieces of grammar helps us evaluate our writing to make it better. Consider motivational speaker Coleman Cox's question, "Now that it's over, what did you really do yesterday that's worth mentioning?" Transfer that thought to how you view your completed writing projects, even the smallest parts, by asking yourself: "Now that I've finished, what did I write that was really worth saying?" Putting phrases, clauses, and conjunctions together correctly, we can make meaningful sentences. And that's why we write!

Match Point

The examples opposite from *O Pioneers!* (1913) give American novelist Willa Cather's (1873–1947) description of the harsh Nebraska frontier. Number your paper from 1 to 10 and correctly match the grammar elements in column A with the examples from column B. While some answers may appear to have more than one correct choice, there is only one best answer for each.

COLUMN **A**	COLUMN **B**
1. coordinating conjunction	**A. Although it was only four o'clock**
2. subordinating conjunction	**B. The light fell upon the two sad young faces**
3. infinitive phrase	**C. that were turned mutely toward it**
4. prepositional phrase	**D. who seemed to be looking with such anguished perplexity**
5. relative pronoun	**E. The homesteads were few and far apart**
6. sentence fragment	**F. here and there a windmill gaunt against the sky**
7. conjunctive adverb	**G. seemed to overwhelm the little beginnings**
8. independent clause	**H. as if it had never been**
9. dependent "that" clause	**I. a sod house crouching in a hollow**
10. participial phrase	**J. But the great fact was the land itself**

ANSWER KEY

GLOSSARY

compound objects: two or more persons or things to which a specified action is directed

compound sentence: a sentence that has two or more independent clauses that are often joined by a comma and a conjunction

compound subject: two or more subjects using the same verb in a sentence

correlate: to have a comparable, shared relationship, as with two correlative conjunctions that are used together (*either* and *or*)

fragment: a group of words that is capitalized and punctuated as a sentence but is an incomplete thought

helping verb: a verb that provides additional help to the main verb (*am, is, are, was, has, have, had,* etc.)

idiom: a group of words that has a different meaning from the definitions of the individual words

inaugural address: a speech made by a U.S. president, marking the beginning of the term of office

literally: using the individual definitions of words to mean exactly what you're saying

main clause: a group of words with a subject and a verb that makes sense by itself and to which other dependent clauses may be connected

object: a person or thing to which a specified action is directed

objective case: the classification of nouns and pronouns that function as receivers of action or as objects of prepositions (*me, us, you, him, her, it, them*)

part of speech: the class or category into which a word may be grouped according to its form changes and its grammatical function; in English, the main parts of speech are verbs, nouns, pronouns, adjectives, adverbs, prepositions, conjunctions, and interjections

participial prepositional phrase: a participle of a verb (such as an *-ing* or *-ed* verb form) that begins a prepositional phrase, a group of words consisting of a preposition, its object, and any modifiers

predicate: the part of a clause or sentence containing a verb and stating something about the subject

punctuation: marks used to provide meaning and separate elements within sentences, such as periods, commas, question marks, exclamation points, semicolons, colons, hyphens, and parentheses

sentence: a unit of expression that contains a subject and a verb and expresses a complete, independent thought

subordinate: to be dependent upon something else; to link a group of words with a subject and verb that cannot stand alone to an independent clause that can

tense: the property of the verb that designates time as present, past, future, or perfect using single-word verbs and auxiliaries (or helping verbs)

SELECTED BIBLIOGRAPHY

The Chicago Manual of Style. 15th ed. Chicago: The University of Chicago Press, 2003.

Darling, Charles. "Guide to Grammar." Capital Community College Foundation. http://grammar.ccc.commnet.edu/grammar/.

Hodges, John C., Winifred B. Horner, Suzanne S. Webb, and Robert K. Miller. *Harbrace College Handbook*. 13th ed. Fort Worth, Tex.: Harcourt Brace College Publishers, 1998.

Hunter, Estelle B., ed. *The New Self-Teaching Course in Practical English and Effective Speech*. Chicago: The Better-Speech Institute of America, 1935.

Lederer, Richard, and Richard Dowis. *Sleeping Dogs Don't Lay: Practical Advice for the Grammatically Challenged*. New York: St. Martin's Press, 1999.

O'Conner, Patricia T. *Woe Is I: The Grammarphobe's Guide to Better English in Plain English*. New York: Riverhead Books, 2004.

———. *Woe Is I Jr.: The Younger Grammarphobe's Guide to Better English*. New York: G. P. Putnam's Sons, 2007.

Warriner, John E., Joseph Mersand, and Francis Griffith. *English Grammar and Composition*. New York: Harcourt, Brace & World, Inc, 1963.

INDEX